Thank You

Dear Parents and Teachers,

We extend our heartfelt gratitude to each of you for choosing our Science of Reading curriculum. Your decision to invest in your child's education is commendable, and we are honored to be a part of their reading journey. At the heart of our curriculum lies the fundamental understanding of phonemic awareness, phonics, and the integration of decodable books, all of which are pivotal in fostering strong literacy skills in young readers. Phonemic awareness forms the basis of understanding how sounds work in words, while phonics provides the essential link between sounds and letters, empowering children to decode words with confidence.

We firmly believe that this curriculum serves as the crucial first step in your child's reading journey, laying down a solid foundation upon which further literacy skills can be built. The incorporation of decodable books ensures that children have access to texts that align closely with the phonics principles they are learning, facilitating a seamless transition from decoding to comprehension. As your child embarks on this exciting adventure of learning to read, rest assured that our curriculum is designed to support their growth every step of the way.

Should you have any questions or require further assistance regarding the curriculum or your child's progress, please do not hesitate to reach out to us at decodabletexts@gmail.com. We are here to support you and your child on this enriching journey towards literacy mastery. Once again, thank you for choosing our Science of Reading curriculum. Together, we can unlock the transformative power of reading in your child's life.

Warm regards,
Adam Free

TABLE OF CONTENTS

Lesson Format

Each lesson will follow the following format. The total length of the lesson should last around thirty minutes. The format and the time breakdown can be seen below.

1. Phonemic awareness (hear it, 5 min)
   a. Isolating.
   b. Blending.
   c. Segmenting.
2. Word and sentence reading (decode it, 5 min)
   a. Read words with the target sound.
   b. Read sentences with the target sound.
3. Decodable book read (read it, 15 min)
   a. Read a decodable text with the target sound.
   b. Reading comprehension (Optional).
   c. Silly sentences.
4. Phonics activities (spell it 5 min)
   a. Spell words with the target sound pattern.
   b. Sound manipulation.

Definitions

- **Phonemic awareness**- Phonemic awareness is the ability to hear and work with the different sounds in spoken words. For example, it's knowing that the word "cat" is made up of the sounds c-a-t, and being able to play around with these sounds.
- **Segmenting-** Segmenting is breaking a word down into its individual sounds. For example, taking the word "dog" and splitting it into its sounds: d-o-g. This helps children learn to read and spell by understanding how different sounds come together to form words.
- **Blending**- Blending is the process of combining individual sounds to form a word. For example, when you hear the sounds b-l-a-ck and put them together to make the word "black."

Definitions

- **Isolating-** Isolating is the ability to pick out a single sound from a word. For example, in the word "sun," isolating the first sound would be hearing the "s" sound on its own.
- **Reading Comprehension Using the 5W's-** For this reading comprehension exercise, students will use the five W's to retell the story. The 5 W's are:
  - Who- Who is the main character or characters?
  - What- what did the main character do?
  - When- When did the story take place?
  - Where- Where did the story take place?
  - Why- Why did the events in the story take place?

Example Script- Isolating

Greet the students and explain the activity: "Today, we're going to play a listening game! We'll listen to some words and figure out what sound each word starts with. All the words we'll use have a short 'a' sound like in 'apple'."

Warm-Up:

- Say the word "cat" slowly and clearly. You can also segment it to model how to get the first sound (c-a-t). Then ask, "What is the first sound you hear in 'cat'?"
- Let the student respond, then confirm, "Yes, it starts with the 'c' sound, which sounds like 'cuh'."

Guided Practice:

- Introduce the next word by saying it clearly: "Listen carefully, 'mat'. What's the first sound in 'mat'?" Again, encourage students to segment the word, especially if they are having trouble (m-a-t).
- Continue with each word in the list.

Example Script- Blending

Greet the students and explain the activity: "Today we're going to play another fun listening game. We will listen to some sounds and put them together to make words. All these words will have the short 'a' sound in the middle, like in 'apple'."

Warm-Up:
- Start by saying the sounds of a simple word slowly and separately. For example, "Listen to these sounds: /c/ /a/ /t/. When we put these sounds together, they make the word 'cat'. Let's say them faster together. C-a-t, Cat. Can you try?"
- Guide the student to say the sounds separately and then blend them to form the word.

Guided Practice:
- Proceed with the next set of sounds. Say, "/m/ /a/ /t/," and then ask, "What word do these sounds make when we put them together?"
- Encourage the student to blend the sounds into the word "mat." Provide feedback as needed.
- Repeat the process with the rest of the words.

Example Script- Segmenting

Greet the students and explain the activity: "Today, we're going to play a sound detective game. We'll take words apart and find out what sounds are in them. All the words we'll use today have a short 'a' sound like in 'hat'."

Warm-Up:
- Start with a simple word. Say, "Let's take the word 'cat'. When we slow it down, we can hear all the sounds that make it up. Listen: 'cat' - /c/ /a/ /t/. Can you say the sounds with me?"
- Have the student repeat the sounds after you, emphasizing each sound.

Guided Practice:
- Introduce the next word, such as "mat." Say, "Now, let's try with 'mat'. What sounds do you hear in 'mat'?"
- Let the student attempt to break the word into sounds. Confirm and correct gently as needed, helping them focus on each distinct sound: /m/ /a/ /t/.
- Continue with more words.

Digraph sh
Set 1

Hear it

Isolating

Ask your student to isolate the **first** sound in each word. Do not allow them to see the words or the book. This is an oral exercise.

- **Bash**
- **Ship**
- **Shut**
- **Dish**
- **Posh**
- **Mesh**

Ask your student to isolate the **middle** sound in each word. Do not allow them to see the words or the book. This is an oral exercise.

- **Cash**
- **Rush**
- **Lip**
- **Sash**
- **Gush**
- **Hush**

Hear it

Isolating

Ask your student to isolate the **last** sound in each word. Do not allow them to see the words or the book. This is an oral exercise.

- **Lush**
- **Shed**
- **Tush**
- **Mut**
- **Ship**
- **Bush**

Hear it

Blending

Ask your student to blend the following sounds into words.

- **B-a-sh**
- **Sh-i-p**
- **Sh-u-t**
- **D-i-sh**
- **P-o-sh**
- **M-e-sh**

Segmenting

Ask your student to break apart the following words into sounds.

- **Cash**
- **Rush**
- **Cash**
- **Mash**
- **Ship**
- **Shut**

Decode it

Word Reading

Ask your student to read the following words.

- Mash
- Ship
- Shut
- Shin
- Gush
- Mesh

Sentence Reading

Ask your student to read the following sentences.

1. Josh has a fish in a dish.
2. The bush in the shed is lush.
3. She will wash the dish.

Read it

Ash is a fish in a big pond. Ash dashes by a lush bush. Ash spots a shell in the mud. He pushes it. A ship gets by Ash and nips him He dashes by in a rush. Ash gets a posh bug to put in a dish. What a lush spot for a fish!

READ IT—THE 5 W'S (OPTIONAL)

Name: _____

Date: _____

Who?	
What?	
When?	
Where?	
Why?	

Read it
Silly Sentences

Ask your student to read the following nonsense words from the box below. Though these are not real words, the goal is to get students to read them fluently and quickly. To accomplish this, you student may try as many times as possible within 3-5 minutes.

1. **Shum fish bash nosh pash.**
2. **Gash shil mosh on lush.**
3. **Shab dash mish kash tush.**
4. **Pish shod gush wosh dish.**
5. **Shig fash nush rish bosh.**

Spell it

Ask your student to spell and write the following words: Mash, Ship, Shin, Gush, Mesh, Bash.

Spell it

Ask your student to write the word in the middle of the page on a white board. Then ask them to change the word into another word, making as few changes as possible. This will likely involve changing only one or two letters. Do not let them see this book while completing this exercise. Ex. Change "mat" into "cat". Change "cat" into "pat". Change "pat" into "pan". Change "pan" into "pad" Etc.

> **Mash**

Cash

Lash

Dash

Rash

Wash

Digraph sh
Set 2

Hear it

Isolating

Ask your student to isolate the **first** sound in each word. Do not allow them to see the words or the book. This is an oral exercise.

- **Hop**
- **Shot**
- **Show**
- **Wash**
- **Sham**
- **Bats**

Ask your student to isolate the **middle** sound in each word. Do not allow them to see the words or the book. This is an oral exercise.

- **Shin**
- **Shaw**
- **Shew**
- **Shad**
- **Mash**
- **Wish**

Hear it

Isolating

Ask your student to isolate the **last** sound in each word. Do not allow them to see the words or the book. This is an oral exercise.

- **Mass**
- **Rash**
- **Sips**

- **Hums**
- **Mush**
- **Shut**

Hear it

Blending

Ask your student to blend the following sounds into words.

- **M-a-sh**
- **P-u-sh**
- **H-a-sh**
- **L-a-sh**
- **S-a-sh**
- **Sh-a-w**

Segmenting

Ask your student to break apart the following words into sounds.

- **Shin**
- **Posh**
- **Shun**
- **Shop**
- **Shew**
- **Ship**

Decode it

Word Reading

Ask your student to read the following words.

- **Shot**
- **Rash**
- **Dish**
- **Shad**
- **Ash**
- **Mush**

Sentence Reading

Ask your student to read the following sentences.

1. **The fish can dash.**
2. **Ash had a rash.**
3. **She has a wish for a dish.**

13

Read it

Josh had a wish to find cash. One day, he saw a bag of cash in the trash. He felt a rush and hid the cash in his dish. But then, his cat, Dash, made a mess and the cash fell. Josh had to wash the cash. Now, he keeps the cash in a jar.

READ IT—THE 5 W'S (OPTIONAL)

Name: _____

Date: _____

Who?	
What?	
When?	
Where?	
Why?	

Read it

Silly Sentences

Ask your student to read the following nonsense words from the box below. Though these are not real words, the goal is to get students to read them fluently and quickly. To accomplish this, you student may try as many times as possible within 3-5 minutes.

1. **Shap the shom on the kish.**
2. **Shab shogs love to shup.**
3. **Sham shan in the shog.**
4. **Shuf the shem with shaz.**
5. **Shig shos shen the shub.**

Spell it

Ask your student to spell and write the following words: Shem, Posh, Dash, Ash, Cash, Mash

___ ___ ___ ___

___ ___ ___ ___

___ ___ ___ ___

___ ___ ___

___ ___ ___ ___

Spell it

Ask your student to write the word in the middle of the page on a white board. Then ask them to change the word into another word, making as few changes as possible. This will likely involve changing only one or two letters. Do not let them see this book while completing this exercise. Ex. Change "mat" into "cat". Change "cat" into "pat". Change "pat" into "pan". Change "pan" into "pad" Etc.

Shop

Shot

Sham

Mash

Wish

Win

Digraph sh
Set 3

Hear it

Isolating

Ask your student to isolate the **first** sound in each word. Do not allow them to see the words or the book. This is an oral exercise.

- **Gash**
- **Hash**
- **Shun**
- **Bush**
- **Shall**
- **Lush**

Ask your student to isolate the **middle** sound in each word. Do not allow them to see the words or the book. This is an oral exercise.

- **Men**
- **Bash**
- **Dish**
- **Mesh**
- **Bun**
- **Shop**

Hear it

Isolating

Ask your student to isolate the **last** sound in each word. Do not allow them to see the words or the book. This is an oral exercise.

- **Cash**
- **Lap**
- **Rush**
- **Sack**
- **Sham**
- **Mush**

Hear it

Blending

Ask your student to blend the following sounds into words.

- **Sh-i-p**
- **Ca-s-h**
- **Sh-o-p**
- **B-u-sh**
- **R-u-sh**
- **P-u-sh**

Segmenting

Ask your student to break apart the following words into sounds.

- **Shed**
- **Lush**
- **Shad**
- **Rash**
- **Mash**
- **Shew**

Decode it

Word Reading

Ask your student to read the following words.

- **Wish**
- **Shum**
- **Gash**
- **Shut**
- **Mesh**
- **Sham**

Sentence Reading

Ask your student to read the following sentences.

1. Josh will bash the mesh with a stick.
2. She has cash and a red sash.
3. The hash in the pan is a sham.

Read it

Mish went to the lush bush by the pond. She saw a big mesh bag stuck in the bush. Mish gave the bush a push and the bag fell. Inside the bag was some cash and a red sash. Mish was glad and took the cash home. She gave the sash to her pal, Jen.

READ IT—THE 5 W'S (OPTIONAL)

Name: _____

Date: _____

Who?	
What?	
When?	
Where?	
Why?	

Read it
Silly Sentences

Ask your student to read the following nonsense words from the box below. Though these are not real words, the goal is to get students to read them fluently and quickly. To accomplish this, you student may try as many times as possible within 3-5 minutes.

1. **Shup the shig in the shom.**
2. **Shem and shok play in the shib.**
3. **Shil finds a shub under a shon.**
4. **Shif likes to shap with the shep.**
5. **Shub the shon on the shid.**

Spell it

Ask your student to spell and write the following words: Cash, Bush, Rush, Gash, Wish.

_____ _____ _____ _____

_____ _____ _____ _____

_____ _____ _____ _____

_____ _____ _____ _____

_____ _____ _____ _____

Spell it

Ask your student to write the word in the middle of the page on a white board. Then ask them to change the word into another word, making as few changes as possible. This will likely involve changing only one or two letters. Do not let them see this book while completing this exercise. Ex. Change "mat" into "cat". Change "cat" into "pat". Change "pat" into "pan". Change "pan" into "pad" Etc.

Ship

Shed

Shash

Lash

Push

Digraph sh
Set 4

Hear it

Isolating

Ask your student to isolate the **first** sound in each word. Do not allow them to see the words or the book. This is an oral exercise.

- **Mush**
- **Shad**
- **Hush**
- **Bash**
- **Shop**
- **Dim**

Ask your student to isolate the **middle** sound in each word. Do not allow them to see the words or the book. This is an oral exercise.

- **Fish**
- **Rush**
- **Gosh**
- **Shun**
- **Sham**
- **Show**

Hear it

Isolating

Ask your student to isolate the **last** sound in each word. Do not allow them to see the words or the book. This is an oral exercise.

- **Shy**
- **Nosh**
- **Jump**
- **Rash**
- **Cape**
- **Mesh**

Hear it

Blending

Ask your student to blend the following sounds into words.

- **Sh-e-d**
- **M-u-sh**
- **G-o-sh**
- **M-a-sh**
- **L-u-sh**
- **H-a-sh**

Segmenting

Ask your student to break apart the following words into sounds.

- **Gosh**
- **Shoe**
- **Shod**
- **She**
- **Shoo**
- **Sham**

Decode it

Word Reading

Ask your student to read the following words.

- **She**
- **Shed**
- **Shin**

- **Shy**
- **Nosh**
- **Shut**

Sentence Reading

Ask your student to read the following sentences.

1. **She has a red ship.**
2. **The shy cat hid.**
3. **His shoe is big.**

Read it

Josh had a red shoe. One day, Josh lost it in the hash. He felt sad and had to rush to look. He saw a bush of mush and a shed. He did not quit. At last, Josh got his shoe in the shed. He ran to show his mom. She gave him a big hug.

READ IT—THE 5 W'S (OPTIONAL)

Name: _____

Date: _____

Who?	
What?	
When?	
Where?	
Why?	

Read it

Silly Sentences

Ask your student to read the following nonsense words from the box below. Though these are not real words, the goal is to get students to read them fluently and quickly. To accomplish this, you student may try as many times as possible within 3-5 minutes.

1. **Shib shix shup shem!**
2. **Shok shib shen shoof.**
3. **Shuv shan shaz shin.**
4. **Shup shig shon shav.**
5. **Shal shud shep shix.**

Spell it

Ask your student to spell and write the following words: Fish, Gosh, Shoe, Shed, She

Spell it

Ask your student to write the word in the middle of the page on a white board. Then ask them to change the word into another word, making as few changes as possible. This will likely involve changing only one or two letters. Do not let them see this book while completing this exercise. Ex. Change "mat" into "cat". Change "cat" into "pat". Change "pat" into "pan". Change "pan" into "pad" Etc.

Shy

Shop

Ship

Tip

Tap

Digraph sh Set 5

Hear it

Isolating

Ask your student to isolate the **first** sound in each word. Do not allow them to see the words or the book. This is an oral exercise.

- **She**
- **Ash**
- **Rat**
- **Van**
- **Hush**
- **Shop**

Ask your student to isolate the **middle** sound in each word. Do not allow them to see the words or the book. This is an oral exercise.

- **Shun**
- **Pin**
- **Fan**
- **Gash**
- **Bed**
- **Pun**

Hear it

Isolating

Ask your student to isolate the **last** sound in each word. Do not allow them to see the words or the book. This is an oral exercise.

- **Fish**
- **Shed**
- **Mash**
- **Lash**
- **Shop**
- **List**

Hear it

Blending

Ask your student to blend the following sounds into words.

- **R-a-sh**
- **Sh-u-n**
- **Sh-o-p**
- **G-a-sh**
- **G-o-sh**
- **M-e-sh**

Segmenting

Ask your student to break apart the following words into sounds.

- **Gosh**
- **Shy**
- **Sham**
- **She**
- **Shea**
- **Shay**

Decode it

Word Reading

Ask your student to read the following words.

- Ship
- Shay
- Shop
- Cash
- Dash
- Mush

Sentence Reading

Ask your student to read the following sentences.

1. The cat **ran and hid in the shed** a rush.
2. I will **hush the pup with a bush.**
3. She had **to push the big box.**

39

Read it

Josh has a shop. His shop sells fish and shells. Each day, Josh will rush to stock the shelves. A big fish tank sits in the shop. Kids love to watch the fish swim and splash. Josh helps them pick a fish. He also has a dish for fish food.

READ IT—THE 5 W'S (OPTIONAL)

Name: _____

Date: _____

Who?	
What?	
When?	
Where?	
Why?	

Read it
Silly Sentences

Ask your student to read the following nonsense words from the box below. Though these are not real words, the goal is to get students to read them fluently and quickly. To accomplish this, you student may try as many times as possible within 3-5 minutes.

1. **Shib shaz a shil.**
2. **Shom shup a shez.**
3. **Shid shem shox sip.**
4. **Shud shim sheb shuz.**
5. **Shal shon shax shep.**

Spell it

Ask your student to spell and write the following words: Sham, Gush, Gosh, Rash, Shin

_____   _____   _____   _____

_____   _____   _____   _____

_____   _____   _____   _____

_____   _____   _____   _____

_____   _____   _____   _____

Spell it

Ask your student to write the word in the middle of the page on a white board. Then ask them to change the word into another word, making as few changes as possible. This will likely involve changing only one or two letters. Do not let them see this book while completing this exercise. Ex. Change "mat" into "cat". Change "cat" into "pat". Change "pat" into "pan". Change "pan" into "pad" Etc.

Sham

Shin

Tin

Tush

Mush

Digraph Th
Set 1

Hear it

Isolating

Ask your student to isolate the **first** sound in each word. Do not allow them to see the words or the book. This is an oral exercise.

- Thin
- Thud
- Tin
- With
- That
- Man

Ask your student to isolate the **middle** sound in each word. Do not allow them to see the words or the book. This is an oral exercise.

- Thus
- Cop
- Them
- Then
- Fit
- Math

Hear it

Isolating

Ask your student to isolate the **last** sound in each word. Do not allow them to see the words or the book. This is an oral exercise.

- Thy
- Then
- Thor
- Math
- Path
- Bath

Hear it

Blending

Ask your student to blend the following sounds into words.

- **Th-i-n**
- **Th-u-d**
- **Th-e-m**
- **Th-aw**
- **Th-a-t**
- **Th-i-s**

Segmenting

Ask your student to break apart the following words into sounds.

- **Thus**
- **Than**
- **Them**
- **Thee**
- **Thou**
- **They**

Decode it

Word Reading

Ask your student to read the following words.

- **They**
- **Them**
- **Thee**

- **Both**
- **Bath**
- **Hath**

Sentence Reading

Ask your student to read the following sentences.

1. **The thin moth sat.**
2. **Beth had a bath.**
3. **That frog is big.**

Read it

A moth sat on a thin stick. The moth had big wings. Beth saw the moth and said, "That moth is fast!" Then, the moth flapped its wings. Beth ran to see the moth. Beth said, "That moth is the best!" The moth then flew off the path with the stick.

READ IT—THE 5 W'S (OPTIONAL)

Name: _____

Date: _____

Who? 	
What?	
When? 	
Where? 	
Why?	

50

Read it
Silly Sentences

Ask your student to read the following nonsense words from the box below. Though these are not real words, the goal is to get students to read them fluently and quickly. To accomplish this, you student may try as many times as possible within 3-5 minutes.

1. **Thip thoz tha blem.**
2. **Rath thub and thix plom.**
3. **Thak thon and thim.**
4. **Doth plath with thub.**
5. **Thes zath blot thig.**

Spell it

Ask your student to spell and write the following words: Then, Them, Thus, Hath, Bath.

Spell it

Ask your student to write the word in the middle of the page on a white board. Then ask them to change the word into another word, making as few changes as possible. This will likely involve changing only one or two letters. Do not let them see this book while completing this exercise. Ex. Change "mat" into "cat". Change "cat" into "pat". Change "pat" into "pan". Change "pan" into "pad" Etc.

Then

Them
Ram
Ran
Bath

Digraph Th

Set 2

Hear it
Isolating

Ask your student to isolate the **first** sound in each word. Do not allow them to see the words or the book. This is an oral exercise.

- **Math**
- **Path**
- **Ruth**
- **Thee**
- **That**
- **This**

Ask your student to isolate the **middle** sound in each word. Do not allow them to see the words or the book. This is an oral exercise.

- **Both**
- **Thud**
- **Then**
- **Goth**
- **Thought**
- **Not**

Hear it

Isolating

Ask your student to isolate the **last** sound in each word. Do not allow them to see the words or the book. This is an oral exercise.

- **Path**
- **Oath**
- **Thin**
- **Thou**
- **Thud**
- **Thaw**

Hear it

Blending

Ask your student to blend the following sounds into words.

- **M-a-th**
- **P-a-th**
- **R-u-th**
- **Th-ee**
- **Th-a-t**
- **Th-i-s**

Segmenting

Ask your student to break apart the following words into sounds.

- **Both**
- **Thud**
- **Then**
- **Goth**
- **Tho**
- **Nth**

Decode it

Word Reading

Ask your student to read the following words.

- **Thou**
- **Then**
- **Thee**
- **Goth**
- **Path**
- **Ruth**

Sentence Reading

Ask your student to read the following sentences.

1. **The thin cat sat with the dog.**
2. **Beth got a bath in the tub.**
3. **Seth will math with the kids.**

Read it

Seth and Beth went on a path. The path was thin and long. They saw a frog in a bath. Seth got a stick and Beth got a twig. They had fun with the things. At the end of the path, they sat and had lunch. The end.

READ IT—THE 5 W'S (OPTIONAL)

Name: _____

Date: _____

Who?	
What?	
When?	
Where?	
Why?	

Read it

Silly Sentences

Ask your student to read the following nonsense words from the box below. Though these are not real words, the goal is to get students to read them fluently and quickly. To accomplish this, you student may try as many times as possible within 3-5 minutes.

1. Thop thed thim thud thaz.
2. Thun thig thal thox thup.
3. Thiz thef thob thuv thit.
4. Thab thom thiv thet thux.
5. Thul thok thap thir theb.

Spell it

Ask your student to spell and write the following words: Ruth, Math, Thud, Path, Thin

Spell it

Ask your student to write the word in the middle of the page on a white board. Then ask them to change the word into another word, making as few changes as possible. This will likely involve changing only one or two letters. Do not let them see this book while completing this exercise. Ex. Change "mat" into "cat". Change "cat" into "pat". Change "pat" into "pan". Change "pan" into "pad" Etc.

Math

Path

Ruth

Both

Goth

Digraph Th
Set 3

Hear it
Isolating

Ask your student to isolate the **first** sound in each word. Do not allow them to see the words or the book. This is an oral exercise.

- **Thin**
- **Myth**
- **That**
- **Fam**
- **Rest**
- **Thud**

Ask your student to isolate the **middle** sound in each word. Do not allow them to see the words or the book. This is an oral exercise.

- **Hath**
- **Thorn**
- **Bud**
- **Then**
- **This**
- **Than**

Hear it

Isolating

Ask your student to isolate the **last** sound in each word. Do not allow them to see the words or the book. This is an oral exercise.

- The
- Thy
- Thee
- Bath
- Both
- Than

Hear it

Blending

Ask your student to blend the following sounds into words.

- **Th-i-n**
- **M-y-th**
- **Th-a-t**
- **Th-ee**
- **P-a-th**
- **Th-u-d**

Segmenting

Ask your student to break apart the following words into sounds.

- **Thug**
- **Thaw**
- **Thud**
- **Then**
- **This**
- **Than**

Decode it

Word Reading

Ask your student to read the following words.

- **Then**
- **Thy**
- **Thin**
- **This**
- **Than**
- **Thee**

Sentence Reading

Ask your student to read the following sentences.

1. **Thad and Beth talk.**
2. **Thum went on the path.**
3. **Then, he hit the thin log.**

Read it

Thad is a math kid. Thad hid in the shed. Meg saw Thad and ran. Thad then took a path to the hill. He had a bag with him. The bag had a big thick moth and a hat. Thad sat on the hill and saw a fish in a thin pond. Thad pets them. Thad is a math kid.

READ IT—THE 5 W'S (OPTIONAL)

Name: _____

Date: _____

Who?	
What?	
When?	
Where?	
Why?	

Read it
Silly Sentences

Ask your student to read the following nonsense words from the box below. Though these are not real words, the goal is to get students to read them fluently and quickly. To accomplish this, you student may try as many times as possible within 3-5 minutes.

1. **Thob the thim.**
2. **Thak and thix.**
3. **Thub thom to thog.**
4. **Thaf theb in thup.**
5. **Thip thel thun thad.**

Spell it

Ask your student to spell and
write the following words:
This, Than, Then, Thy, Path

_ _ _ _

_ _ _ _

_ _ _ _

_ _ _ _

_ _ _ _

Spell it

Ask your student to write the word in the middle of the page on a white board. Then ask them to change the word into another word, making as few changes as possible. This will likely involve changing only one or two letters. Do not let them see this book while completing this exercise. Ex. Change "mat" into "cat". Change "cat" into "pat". Change "pat" into "pan". Change "pan" into "pad" Etc.

Then

Them

Thug

Thin

This

Digraph Th
Set 4

Hear it

Isolating

Ask your student to isolate the **first** sound in each word. Do not allow them to see the words or the book. This is an oral exercise.

- **Oath**
- **Both**
- **Gum**
- **With**
- **Thus**
- **Thew**

Ask your student to isolate the **middle** sound in each word. Do not allow them to see the words or the book. This is an oral exercise.

- **Thin**
- **Dig**
- **Them**
- **Thus**
- **Than**
- **Team**

Hear it

Isolating

Ask your student to isolate the **last** sound in each word. Do not allow them to see the words or the book. This is an oral exercise.

- **Hath**
- **Math**
- **Then**
- **The**
- **With**
- **Pack**

Hear it

Blending

Ask your student to blend the following sounds into words.

- **M-a-th**
- **B-o-th**
- **G-o-th**
- **W-i-th**
- **Th-u-s**
- **H-a-th**

Segmenting

Ask your student to break apart the following words into sounds.

- **Thin**
- **Thou**
- **Them**
- **Thus**
- **Than**
- **This**

Decode it

Word Reading

Ask your student to read the following words.

- **Both**
- **Goth**
- **Pith**
- **Math**
- **Hath**
- **Them**

Sentence Reading

Ask your student to read the following sentences.

1. **The thin moth sat with Seth.**
2. **Beth has math with Ruth.**
3. **Both kids will play with the ball**

Read it

Ruth is a girl. She has a thin cat. The cat is with Ruth in the path. Ruth sits with her cat on a thick bench. They both watch the moths thud by. Ruth's hat is big and black. Thus, the cat naps on Ruth's lap. Ruth thinks this is the best day. Both of them sit and think that this is the best day.

READ IT—THE 5 W'S (OPTIONAL)

Name: _____

Date: _____

Who?	
What?	
When?	
Where?	
Why?	

Spell it

Ask your student to spell and write the following words:
Path, Thick, Think, Thin, Ruth

Spell it

Ask your student to write the word in the middle of the page on a white board. Then ask them to change the word into another word, making as few changes as possible. This will likely involve changing only one or two letters. Do not let them see this book while completing this exercise. Ex. Change "mat" into "cat". Change "cat" into "pat". Change "pat" into "pan". Change "pan" into "pad" Etc.

Pith

Path

Math

Them

Think

Digraph Th

Set 5

Hear it

Isolating

Ask your student to isolate the **first** sound in each word. Do not allow them to see the words or the book. This is an oral exercise.

- **Doth**
- **Pan**
- **Moth**
- **Path**
- **Yam**
- **Both**

Ask your student to isolate the **middle** sound in each word. Do not allow them to see the words or the book. This is an oral exercise.

- **Then**
- **Thine**
- **Thick**
- **Most**
- **Last**
- **Pox**

Hear it

Isolating

Ask your student to isolate the **last** sound in each word. Do not allow them to see the words or the book. This is an oral exercise.

- **Than**
- **Hath**
- **Thee**
- **Thy**
- **Then**
- **They**

Hear it

Blending

Ask your student to blend the following sounds into words.

- **D-o-th**
- **P-i-th**
- **M-o-th**
- **P-a-th**
- **Th-a-n**
- **B-o-th**

Segmenting

Ask your student to break apart the following words into sounds.

- **The**
- **Thy**
- **Tho**
- **That**
- **Then**
- **Them**

Decode it

Word Reading

Ask your student to read the following words.

- **Than**
- **Hath**
- **Thee**

- **Path**
- **Seth**
- **Both**

Sentence Reading

Ask your student to read the following sentences.

1. **The moth doth rest on the pith.**
2. **Seth and Beth both saw the bath.**
3. **With a sigh, Ruth held the oath.**

Read it

Seth and Beth went to the path by the lake. They saw a big moth on a thick log. Beth said, "Look, Seth! The moth doth rest." Seth and Beth sat with the moth. They both had fun. Then, they saw a fish with a thin fin. "This is the best day," said Beth.

READ IT—THE 5 W'S (OPTIONAL)

Name: _____

Date: _____

Who?	
What?	
When?	
Where?	
Why?	

Spell it

Ask your student to spell and write the following words: Doth, Seth, Beth, Thin, Then, Them.

Spell it

Ask your student to write the word in the middle of the page on a white board. Then ask them to change the word into another word, making as few changes as possible. This will likely involve changing only one or two letters. Do not let them see this book while completing this exercise. Ex. Change "mat" into "cat". Change "cat" into "pat". Change "pat" into "pan". Change "pan" into "pad" Etc.

Doth

Hath

Moth

Seth

Beth

Digraph Ch/Tch Set 1

Hear it

Isolating

Ask your student to isolate the **first** sound in each word. Do not allow them to see the words or the book. This is an oral exercise.

- **Chit**
- **Mill**
- **Chug**
- **Fit**
- **Chef**
- **Mach**

Ask your student to isolate the **middle** sound in each word. Do not allow them to see the words or the book. This is an oral exercise.

- **Aching**
- **Bach**
- **Chip**
- **Poch**
- **Such**
- **Luck**

Hear it

Isolating

Ask your student to isolate the **last** sound in each word. Do not allow them to **see the** words or the **book**. This is an oral **exercise**.

- Itch
- Chewy
- Much
- Chad
- Arch
- Mach

Hear it

Blending

Ask your student to blend the following sounds into words.

- **Ch-i-t**
- **Ch-u-m**
- **Ch-u-g**
- **Ch-a-d**
- **Ch-e-f**
- **M-a-ch**

Segmenting

Ask your student to break apart the following words into sounds.

- **Ache**
- **Bach**
- **Chap**
- **Poch**
- **Such**
- **Lich**

Decode it

Word Reading

Ask your student to read the following words.

- **Chum**
- **Much**
- **Dutch**
- **Chip**
- **Itch**
- **Itchy**

Sentence Reading

Ask your student to read the following sentences.

1. **Chad will chop the log.**
2. **The chip is on the mat.**
3. **Catch the fish in the pond.**

Read it

Chad the bug sat on a Dutch log. He saw a chip and began to chat. Chad did a hop to the chip to chop the log. A chill chick came by and saw Chad. The chick did not like itchy bugs. Chad had to run fast to a log patch. The chick did a peck, but Chad hid in the thick grass.

READ IT—THE 5 W'S (OPTIONAL)

Name: _____

Date: _____

Who? 	
What?	
When?	
Where? 	
Why?	

Read it

Silly Sentences

Ask your student to read the following nonsense words from the box below. Though these are not real words, the goal is to get students to read them fluently and quickly. To accomplish this, you student may try as many times as possible within 3-5 minutes.

1. **Chog the chub, chimed chee.**
2. **Chub chex chots, chel chay.**
3. **Chiv chop chuz, chot chim.**
4. **Chix chub chon, chot chel.**
5. **Chup chaz chib, chee chov.**

Spell it

Ask your student to spell and write the following words: Chit, Chat, Chum, Chad, Itch.

_____ _____ _____ _____

_____ _____ _____ _____

_____ _____ _____ _____

_____ _____ _____ _____

_____ _____ _____ _____

Spell it

Ask your student to write the word in the middle of the page on a white board. Then ask them to change the word into another word, making as few changes as possible. This will likely involve changing only one or two letters. Do not let them see this book while completing this exercise. Ex. Change "mat" into "cat". Change "cat" into "pat". Change "pat" into "pan". Change "pan" into "pad" Etc.

Chit

Chat

Chin

Chill

Chick

Digraph Ch/Tch
Set 2

Hear it

Isolating

Ask your student to isolate the **first** sound in each word. Do not allow them to see the words or the book. This is an oral exercise.

- **Chat**
- **Mist**
- **Chop**
- **Lack**
- **Chew**
- **Rich**

Ask your student to isolate the **middle** sound in each word. Do not allow them to see the words or the book. This is an oral exercise.

- **Much**
- **Such**
- **Wrist**
- **Well**
- **Lug**
- **Match**

Hear it

Isolating

Ask your student to isolate the **last** sound in each word. Do not allow them to see the words or the book. This is an oral exercise.

- Chip
- Loch
- Chick
- Etch
- Ouch
- Rich

Hear it

Blending

Ask your student to blend the following sounds into words.

- **Ch-a-t**
- **Ch-i-p**
- **Ch-o-p**
- **Ch-i-n**
- **Ch-ew**
- **R-i-ch**

Segmenting

Ask your student to break apart the following words into sounds.

- **Much**
- **Such**
- **Arch**
- **Inch**
- **Each**
- **Itch**

Decode it

Word Reading

Ask your student to read the following words.

- Etch
- Rich
- Stitch
- Chin
- Chum
- Chop

Sentence Reading

Ask your student to read the following sentences.

1. Chad will chat with his chum.
2. The chick is wet.
3. Check the blue box.

100

Read it

Chip is a child. Chip has a chat with a chum. They check the map and plan fun. Chip packs a lunch. They munch on chips and a peach. Chip and the chum find a rich patch of grass. They sit and chat in the sun. The child is glad. It is a chill day!

READ IT—THE 5 W'S (OPTIONAL)

Name: _____

Date: _____

Who?	
What?	
When?	
Where?	
Why?	

Read it
Silly Sentences

Ask your student to read the following nonsense words from the box below. Though these are not real words, the goal is to get students to read them fluently and quickly. To accomplish this, you student may try as many times as possible within 3-5 minutes.

1. **The chib chuffed a chog in the chat.**
2. **Chit chomps on a chud with chicks.**
3. **The chug cheshed a chub in the chal.**
4. **Chas chacks a chon on chaff.**
5. **The chimp chuts a chax in the chop.**

Spell it

Ask your student to spell and write the following words: Etch, Rich, Chin, Chad, Check.

Spell it

Ask your student to write the word in the middle of the page on a white board. Then ask them to change the word into another word, making as few changes as possible. This will likely involve changing only one or two letters. Do not let them see this book while completing this exercise. Ex. Change "mat" into "cat". Change "cat" into "pat". Change "pat" into "pan". Change "pan" into "pad" Etc.

Chop

Check

Etch

Inch

Rich

Digraph Ch/Tch Set 3

Hear it

Isolating

Ask your student to isolate the **first** sound in each word. Do not allow them to see the words or the book. This is an oral exercise.

- **Char**
- **Bach**
- **Chicken**
- **Bill**
- **Chug**
- **Vat**

Ask your student to isolate the **middle** sound in each word. Do not allow them to see the words or the book. This is an oral exercise.

- **Rich**
- **Chap**
- **Such**
- **Chew**
- **Mach**
- **Much**

Hear it

Isolating

Ask your student to isolate the **last** sound in each word. Do not allow them to **see the** words or the **book**. This is an oral **exercise.**

- Chin
- Chat
- Chop
- Arch
- Chap
- Such

Hear it

Blending

Ask your student to blend the following sounds into words.

- **S-u-ch**
- **B-a-ch**
- **I-n-ch**
- **W-a-tch**
- **H-a-tch**
- **Ch-e-f**

Segmenting

Ask your student to break apart the following words into sounds.

- **Rich**
- **Chap**
- **Watch**
- **Bench**
- **Mach**
- **Much**

Decode it

Word Reading

Ask your student to read the following words.

- **Chin**
- **Chap**
- **Watch**
- **Chuck**
- **Punch**
- **Witch**

Sentence Reading

Ask your student to read the following sentences.

1. **Chuck will catch the fish.**
2. **The chick pecks at the chip.**
3. **Check if the chair is red**

Read it

Chuck is a chef. He chops fish and makes rich chub. Chuck checks each dish. He puts a bunch of chips on the top of the chub. The chef likes to chat while he cooks. His chum, Chip, helps with lunch. They make a bunch of food. The fish and chips are a hit!

READ IT—THE 5 W'S (OPTIONAL)

Name: _____

Date: _____

Who? 	
What? 	
When? 	
Where? 	
Why? 	

Read it
Silly Sentences

Ask your student to read the following nonsense words from the box below. Though these are not real words, the goal is to get students to read them fluently and quickly. To accomplish this, you student may try as many times as possible within 3-5 minutes.

1. Chib chon chep chub chad.
2. Chep chit chog chim chux.
3. Chub choz chif chud chak.
4. Chaz chul chot chib chag.
5. Chik chon chet chob chad.

Spell it

Ask your student to spell and write the following words: Chum, Chub, Chef, Much, Bunch.

Spell it

Ask your student to write the word in the middle of the page on a white board. Then ask them to change the word into another word, making as few changes as possible. This will likely involve changing only one or two letters. Do not let them see this book while completing this exercise. Ex. Change "mat" into "cat". Change "cat" into "pat". Change "pat" into "pan". Change "pan" into "pad" Etc.

Bach

Much

Such

Chub

Chum

Digraph Ch/Tch Set 4

Hear it

Isolating

Ask your student to isolate the **first** sound in each word. Do not allow them to see the words or the book. This is an oral exercise.

- Such
- Each
- Much
- Chuck
- Inch
- Chad

Ask your student to isolate the **middle** sound in each word. Do not allow them to see the words or the book. This is an oral exercise.

- Chew
- Chin
- Mill
- Chum
- Men
- Zip

Hear it

Isolating

Ask your student to isolate the **last** sound in each word. Do not allow them to see the words or the book. This is an oral exercise.

- **Chug**
- **Chef**
- **Lunch**
- **Match**
- **Chit**
- **Itch**

Hear it

Blending

Ask your student to blend the following sounds into words.

- **S-u-ch**
- **Ea-ch**
- **M-u-ch**
- **Ar-ch**
- **I-n-ch**
- **Watch**

Segmenting

Ask your student to break apart the following words into sounds.

- **Chew**
- **Chin**
- **Chug**
- **Chum**
- **Chap**
- **Chow**

Decode it

Word Reading

Ask your student to read the following words.

- Catch
- Match
- Much
- Such
- Chit
- Chat

Sentence Reading

Ask your student to read the following sentences.

1. The rich **man** can catch **a big** fish.
2. Chip will **go up** such a hill.
3. Chad will **munch on a thick bun.**

Read it

Chic is a rich cat. She likes to sit on a thick ditch. Chic will munch on fish and chips. Chad and Chip, her pals, like to play catch. They run and jump by the bench. Chic will watch from the ditch. Chic, Chad, and Chip bunch up by the chest.

READ IT—THE 5 W'S (OPTIONAL)

Name: _____

Date: _____

Who?	
What?	
When?	
Where?	
Why?	

Read it
Silly Sentences

Ask your student to read the following nonsense words from the box below. Though these are not real words, the goal is to get students to read them fluently and quickly. To accomplish this, you student may try as many times as possible within 3-5 minutes.

1. Chog the chub with a chix.
2. Chum ched and chaz a chot.
3. Chib chon and chat the chuf.
4. Chik chops a chot of chus.
5. Chof chad a chub in the chal.

Spell it

Ask your student to spell and write the following words: Inch, Much, Munch, Lunch, Catch.

____ ____ ____ ____

____ ____ ____ ____

____ ____ ____ ____ ____

____ ____ ____ ____ ____

____ ____ ____ ____ ____

Spell it

Ask your student to write the word in the middle of the page on a white board. Then ask them to change the word into another word, making as few changes as possible. This will likely involve changing only one or two letters. Do not let them see this book while completing this exercise. Ex. Change "mat" into "cat". Change "cat" into "pat". Change "pat" into "pan". Change "pan" into "pad" Etc.

Munch

Lunch

Hunch

Chum

Chimp

Digraph Ch/Tch Set 5

Hear it

Isolating

Ask your student to isolate the **first** sound in each word. Do not allow them to see the words or the book. This is an oral exercise.

- **Chia**
- **Which**
- **Chap**
- **Liam**
- **Run**
- **Itch**

Ask your student to isolate the **middle** sound in each word. Do not allow them to see the words or the book. This is an oral exercise.

- **Itchy**
- **Lad**
- **Name**
- **Fine**
- **Chill**
- **Dad**

Hear it

Isolating

Ask your student to isolate the **last** sound in each word. Do **not** allow them to **see the** words or the **book**. This is an oral **exercise**.

- **Chum**
- **Charm**
- **Catch**
- **List**
- **Fun**
- **Latch**

Hear it

Blending

Ask your student to blend the following sounds into words.

- **L-a-tch**
- **H-u-n-ch**
- **Ch-a-p**
- **P-u-n-ch**
- **W-a-tch**
- **P-i-n-ch**

Segmenting

Ask your student to break apart the following words into sounds.

- **Etch**
- **Punch**
- **Chad**
- **Latch**
- **Chip**
- **Pinch**

Decode it

Word Reading

Ask your student to read the following words.

- **Ouch**
- **Etch**
- **Chap**

- **Inch**
- **Itch**
- **Chia**

Sentence Reading

Ask your student to read the following sentences.

1. **Chit and chat with the chum.**
2. **Chug the hot cup of chai.**
3. **Chop the big, red chip.**

Read it

Chip the chick sat on a bench. He had pinch of lunch with Rich. The bunch had chips to munch on. The bunch then had a hunch. Chip and Rich went to catch fish at the beach. Rich got a chunk of fish. Chip got a bunch of fish. They had fun in the sun and felt like champs.

READ IT—THE 5 W'S (OPTIONAL)

Name: _____

Date: _____

Who?	
What? 	
When?	
Where? 	
Why?	

Read it
Silly Sentences

Ask your student to read the following nonsense words from the box below. Though these are not real words, the goal is to get students to read them fluently and quickly. To accomplish this, you student may try as many times as possible within 3-5 minutes.

1. **Chib chot a chuz chog.**
2. **Chif chus the chim chub.**
3. **Chok and chab met chig.**
4. **Chud chaz a chon chum.**
5. **Chep chad a chiv chin.**

Spell it

Ask your student to spell and write the following words: Chunk, Hunch, Munch, Champ, Champs

-- -- -- -- --

-- -- -- -- --

-- -- -- -- --

-- -- -- -- --

-- -- -- -- --

Spell it

Ask your student to write the word in the middle of the page on a white board. Then ask them to change the word into another word, making as few changes as possible. This will likely involve changing only one or two letters. Do not let them see this book while completing this exercise. Ex. Change "mat" into "cat". Change "cat" into "pat". Change "pat" into "pan". Change "pan" into "pad" Etc.

> ## Munch

Pinch

Bench

Hunch

Lunch

Digraph Ck Set 1

Hear it

Isolating

Ask your student to isolate the **first** sound in each word. Do not allow them to see the words or the book. This is an oral exercise.

- **Back**
- **Lick**
- **Deck**
- **Fact**
- **Hack**
- **Latch**

Ask your student to isolate the **middle** sound in each word. Do not allow them to see the words or the book. This is an oral exercise.

- **Kick**
- **Lick**
- **Luck**
- **Mock**
- **Neck**
- **Pack**

Hear it

Isolating

Ask your student to isolate the **last** sound in each word. Do not allow them to see the words or the book. This is an oral exercise.

- **Pick**
- **Stim**
- **Ick**
- **John**
- **Rock**
- **Mom**

Hear it

Blending

Ask your student to blend the following sounds into words.

- **B-a-ck**
- **B-u-ck**
- **D-e-ck**
- **D-o-ck**
- **H-a-ck**
- **J-a-ck**

Segmenting

Ask your student to break apart the following words into sounds.

- **Kick**
- **Lick**
- **Luck**
- **Mock**
- **Neck**
- **Pack**

Decode it
Word Reading

Ask your student to read the following words.

- Duck
- Buck
- Deck
- Rock
- Jack
- Kick

Sentence Reading

Ask your student to read the following sentences.

1. Jack will pack a sack.
2. The duck is back.
3. Rick can kick the rock.

Read it

Jack had a rock. It was thick and black. He kept it in his pack. One day, Rick saw the rock. "Can I see the black rock?" Rick asked. Jack gave Rick the rock quickly. Rick felt the thick rock. "It is slick!" Rick said. They put the rock back in the pack.

READ IT—THE 5 W'S (OPTIONAL)

Name: _____

Date: _____

Who?	
What?	
When?	
Where?	
Why?	

Read it
Silly Sentences

Ask your student to read the following nonsense words from the box below. Though these are not real words, the goal is to get students to read them fluently and quickly. To accomplish this, you student may try as many times as possible within 3-5 minutes.

1. **The zock pack by the smick.**
2. **A fick zock the plack.**
3. **Zick nock a guck on a vick.**
4. **Muck bluck a snick wack.**
5. **Thuck rick a jock on a zock.**

Spell it

Ask your student to spell and write the following words: Rock, Jack, Kick, Buck, Duck.

____ ____ ____ ____

____ ____ ____ ____

____ ____ ____ ____

____ ____ ____ ____

____ ____ ____ ____

Spell it

Ask your student to write the word in the middle of the page on a white board. Then ask them to change the word into another word, making as few changes as possible. This will likely involve changing only one or two letters. Do not let them see this book while completing this exercise. Ex. Change "mat" into "cat". Change "cat" into "pat". Change "pat" into "pan". Change "pan" into "pad" Etc.

Rock

Jack

Kick

Lick

Luck

Digraph Ck
Set 2

Hear it

Isolating

Ask your student to isolate the **first** sound in each word. Do not allow them to see the words or the book. This is an oral exercise.

- Rock
- Sick
- Suck
- Tick
- Wick
- Beck

Ask your student to isolate the **middle** sound in each word. Do not allow them to see the words or the book. This is an oral exercise.

- Duck
- Pin
- Jock
- Lack
- June
- Nock

Hear it

Isolating

Ask your student to isolate the **last** sound in each word. Do not allow them to see the words or the book. This is an oral exercise.

- Lack
- Gum
- Tuck
- Fan
- Puck
- Sack

Hear it

Blending

Ask your student to blend the following sounds into words.

- **R-o-ck**
- **S-i-ck**
- **S-u-ck**
- **T-i-ck**
- **W-i-ck**
- **B-e-ck**

Segmenting

Ask your student to break apart the following words into sounds.

- **Duck**
- **Neck**
- **Jock**
- **Lack**
- **Lock**
- **Nock**

Decode it

Word Reading

Ask your student to read the following words.

- **Lack**
- **Muck**
- **Neck**
- **Jock**
- **Tick**
- **Rack**

Sentence Reading

Ask your student to read the following sentences.

1. **Nick can kick the ball.**
2. **The clock went tick tock.**
3. **Pick up the black sock.**

Read it

Ron is a jock. He likes to chuck and kick sticks. One day, Ron got a new sack. In the sack, he got a rock, a deck, a snack, and a duck. The duck quacked and made Ron crack up. He packed the sack in his pocket and went to the park. Ron's best trick is an attack kick.

READ IT—THE 5 W'S (OPTIONAL)

Name: _____

Date: _____

Who?	
What?	
When?	
Where?	
Why?	

Read it

Silly Sentences

Ask your student to read the following nonsense words from the box below. Though these are not real words, the goal is to get students to read them fluently and quickly. To accomplish this, you student may try as many times as possible within 3-5 minutes.

1. **The crick zock got stuck in a wock.**
2. **Pluck the dack in the wocky rack.**
3. **Flock the tick with a smock on the deck.**
4. **Juck and keck at the lick zocky tock.**
5. **Zick the muck in the backy quack.**

Spell it

Ask your student to spell and write the following words: Jock, Kick, Sack, Duck, Chuck.

Spell it

Ask your student to write the word in the middle of the page on a white board. Then ask them to change the word into another word, making as few changes as possible. This will likely involve changing only one or two letters. Do not let them see this book while completing this exercise. Ex. Change "mat" into "cat". Change "cat" into "pat". Change "pat" into "pan". Change "pan" into "pad" Etc.

Duck

Neck

Tuck

Jock

Sick

Digraph Ck

Set 3

Hear it

Isolating

Ask your student to isolate the **first** sound in each word. Do not allow them to see the words or the book. This is an oral exercise.

- **Pock**
- **Sack**
- **Fist**
- **Tack**
- **Dim**
- **Rim**

Ask your student to isolate the **middle** sound in each word. Do not allow them to see the words or the book. This is an oral exercise.

- **Buck**
- **Back**
- **Dock**
- **Deck**
- **Kick**
- **Hack**

Hear it

Isolating

Ask your student to isolate the **last** sound in each word. Do not allow them to see the words or the book. This is an oral exercise.

- **Him**
- **Lick**
- **Luck**
- **Still**
- **Rock**
- **Ick**

Hear it

Blending

Ask your student to blend the following sounds into words.

- **P-i-ck**
- **S-a-ck**
- **S-o-ck**
- **T-a-ck**
- **T-u-ck**
- **Y-u-ck**

Segmenting

Ask your student to break apart the following words into sounds.

- **Buck**
- **Back**
- **Dock**
- **Deck**
- **Kick**
- **Hack**

Decode it

Word Reading

Ask your student to read the following words.

- **Tack**
- **Sack**
- **Yuck**
- **Back**
- **Kick**
- **Dock**

Sentence Reading

Ask your student to read the following sentences.

1. **The duck's quack is lucky.**
2. **Pack the sack with snacks.**
3. **He will kick the rock.**

Read it

Rick went to the pond to see the muck. He had a big stick and a black sack. He smacks the muck with his stick. The muck was thick and stuck to the stick. Rick put the muck in his sack. He took the sack back to his shack. Now Rick had muck to chuck. What luck!

READ IT—THE 5 W'S (OPTIONAL)

Name: _____

Date: _____

Who?	
What?	
When?	
Where?	
Why?	

Read it
Silly Sentences

Ask your student to read the following nonsense words from the box below. Though these are not real words, the goal is to get students to read them fluently and quickly. To accomplish this, you student may try as many times as possible within 3-5 minutes.

1. **The zock clack when the puck hit it.**
2. **Mick and Jick yuck at the big yock.**
3. **Flick the muck to the quack in the ack.**
4. **Slock the wock on the thick back.**
5. **The zick Deck in the black sack.**

Spell it

Ask your student to spell and write the following words: Tack, Suck, Yuck, Kick, Back, Sock

Spell it

Ask your student to write the word in the middle of the page on a white board. Then ask them to change the word into another word, making as few changes as possible. This will likely involve changing only one or two letters. Do not let them see this book while completing this exercise. Ex. Change "mat" into "cat". Change "cat" into "pat". Change "pat" into "pan". Change "pan" into "pad" Etc.

Pock

Sack

Sock

Tack

Tuck

Digraph Ck
Set 4

Hear it

Isolating

Ask your student to isolate the **first** sound in each word. Do not allow them to see the words or the book. This is an oral exercise.

- **Pick**
- **Rick**
- **Date**
- **Lack**
- **Light**
- **Mock**

Ask your student to isolate the **middle** sound in each word. Do not allow them to see the words or the book. This is an oral exercise.

- **Hen**
- **Back**
- **Fine**
- **Yuck**
- **Gate**
- **Pick**

Hear it

Isolating

Ask your student to isolate the **last** sound in each word. Do not allow them to see the words or the book. This is an oral exercise.

- Duck
- Game
- Wick
- Fill
- Jack
- Tack

Hear it

Blending

Ask your student to blend the following sounds into words.

- **P-i-ck**
- **R-i-ck**
- **R-a-ck**
- **L-a-ck**
- **N-e-ck**
- **M-o-ck**

Segmenting

Ask your student to break apart the following words into sounds.

- **Ack**
- **Back**
- **Bucket**
- **Yuck**
- **Lucky**
- **Pocket**

Decode it

Word Reading

Ask your student to read the following words.

- **Pack**
- **Ack**
- **Rick**
- **Neck**
- **Mock**
- **Buck**

Sentence Reading

Ask your student to read the following sentences.

1. **Rick got stuck.**
2. **Pick the rocket in the pocket.**
3. **Jack got stuck in the muck**

Read it

A buck ran into the thick. He was quick and slick. Nick saw the buck and was in shock. He had a big step back. "Check out that buck," Nick said. The buck looked back at Nick and then ran. Nick went to the thick to check out the buck. He saw the buck jump over a rock.

READ IT—THE 5 W'S (OPTIONAL)

Name: _____

Date: _____

Who?	
What? 	
When?	
Where? 	
Why? 	

Read it

Silly Sentences

Ask your student to read the following nonsense words from the box below. Though these are not real words, the goal is to get students to read them fluently and quickly. To accomplish this, you student may try as many times as possible within 3-5 minutes.

1. Zick the mack cluck in an ack.
2. Bock and leck ruck the zick.
3. Wick, yuck, and tock gack in muck.
4. Tuck the jock at the vick lack.
5. Dack, fick, and hack pluck a zock.

Spell it

Ask your student to spell and write the following words: Buck, Back, Nick, Mock, Lack,

Spell it

Ask your student to write the word in the middle of the page on a white board. Then ask them to change the word into another word, making as few changes as possible. This will likely involve changing only one or two letters. Do not let them see this book while completing this exercise. Ex. Change "mat" into "cat". Change "cat" into "pat". Change "pat" into "pan". Change "pan" into "pad" Etc.

Lack

Pack

Pick

Nick

Rick

Digraph Ck

Set 5

Hear it

Isolating

Ask your student to isolate the **first** sound in each word. Do not allow them to see the words or the book. This is an oral exercise.

- **Pock**
- **Nock**
- **Hack**
- **Lick**
- **Suck**
- **Wack**

Ask your student to isolate the **middle** sound in each word. Do not allow them to see the words or the book. This is an oral exercise.

- **Wick**
- **Tock**
- **Won**
- **Puck**
- **Sick**
- **Sap**

Hear it

Isolating

Ask your student to isolate the **last** sound in each word. Do not allow them to see the words or the book. This is an oral exercise.

- **Sap**
- **Sack**
- **Gate**
- **Bob**
- **Duck**
- **Heal**

Hear it

Blending

Ask your student to blend the following sounds into words.

- **P-o-ck**
- **N-o-ck**
- **H-a-ck**
- **L-i-ck**
- **S-u-ck**
- **W-a-ck**

Segmenting

Ask your student to break apart the following words into sounds.

- **Wick**
- **Tock**
- **Jock**
- **Puck**
- **Sick**
- **Tick**

Decode it
Word Reading

Ask your student to read the following words.

- Puck
- Suck
- Nock
- Tick
- Tock
- Tack

Sentence Reading

Ask your student to read the following sentences.

1. Nick can kick the rock.
2. Zack will stack the blocks.
3. Mick had a snack in the truck.

172

Read it

Nick and Zack go to the dock. Both pack a snack in a pocket. At the dock, they see a duck and a big rock. Nick can kick the rock into the stack. Zack checks the clock. They have fun at the dock. The duck quacks, and they crack up. It is time to go back home.

READ IT—THE 5 W'S (OPTIONAL)

Name: _____

Date: _____

Who?	
What?	
When?	
Where?	
Why?	

Read it
Silly Sentences

Ask your student to read the following nonsense words from the box below. Though these are not real words, the goal is to get students to read them fluently and quickly. To accomplish this, you student may try as many times as possible within 3-5 minutes.

1. **Zick the duck nock the click.**
2. **Flick the muck and juck it back.**
3. **Tock the sack and mock the zick.**
4. **Puck the wick and leck the ruck.**
5. **Wick the bon and tack the nick.**

Spell it

Ask your student to spell and write the following words:
Nick, Zack, Dock, Rock, Duck.

Spell it

Ask your student to write the word in the middle of the page on a white board. Then ask them to change the word into another word, making as few changes as possible. This will likely involve changing only one or two letters. Do not let them see this book while completing this exercise. Ex. Change "mat" into "cat". Change "cat" into "pat". Change "pat" into "pan". Change "pan" into "pad" Etc.

Rick

Zack

Rock

Dock

Back

Digraph Qu Set 1

Hear it

Isolating

Ask your student to isolate the **first** sound in each word. Do not allow them to see the words or the book. This is an oral exercise.

- **Quip**
- **Quiz**
- **Rip**
- **Last**
- **Quad**
- **Fig**

Ask your student to isolate the **middle** sound in each word. Do not allow them to see the words or the book. This is an oral exercise.

- **Jim**
- **Quick**
- **Quell**
- **Bail**
- **Plack**
- **Drum**

Hear it

Isolating

Ask your student to isolate the **last** sound in each word. Do **not** allow them to **see the** words or the **book**. This is an oral **exercise**.

- **Quill**
- **Quad**
- **Drank**
- **Flip**
- **Shack**
- **Quid**

Hear it

Blending

Ask your student to blend the following sounds into words.

- **Qu-i-p**
- **Qu-i-z**
- **Qu-i-t**
- **Qu-i-ck**
- **Qu-a-d**
- **Qu-e-s-t**

Segmenting

Ask your student to break apart the following words into sounds.

- **Quip**
- **Quiz**
- **Quit**
- **Quick**
- **Quad**
- **Quest**

Decode it

Word Reading

Ask your student to read the following words.

- **Quit**
- **Quick**
- **Quilt**
- **Squad**
- **Quell**
- **Quill**

Sentence Reading

Ask your student to read the following sentences.

1. **The quid fell quick.**
2. **The quest is back on.**
3. **We quiz Tom on the quad.**

Read it

A quail had a nest by a quiet quad. One day, she dug in the sand for a squad of bugs. It was a quest. The quail did not quit her quest. She wanted to be the queen of the squad. A dog ran by to quell the Qail's quest. But she did not stop. The quail had to equip and shovel. She soon got the squad of bugs. The quail was a queen.

READ IT—THE 5 W'S (OPTIONAL)

Name: _____

Date: _____

Who?	
What?	
When?	
Where?	
Why?	

Read it

Silly Sentences

Ask your student to read the following nonsense words from the box below. Though these are not real words, the goal is to get students to read them fluently and quickly. To accomplish this, you student may try as many times as possible within 3-5 minutes.

1. **Quib the quix quat.**
2. **Quon the quoff quex.**
3. **Quaf the quop quiz.**
4. **Quet the quub quip.**
5. **Quig the quaz quib.**

Spell it
Ask your student to spell and write the following words:
Quit, Quip, Quiz, Quest, Quill.

Spell it

Ask your student to write the word in the middle of the page on a white board. Then ask them to change the word into another word, making as few changes as possible. This will likely involve changing only one or two letters. Do not let them see this book while completing this exercise. Ex. Change "mat" into "cat". Change "cat" into "pat". Change "pat" into "pan". Change "pan" into "pad" Etc.

Quid

Quit

Quiz

Quill

Quell

Digraph Qu

Set 2

Hear it

Isolating

Ask your student to isolate the **first** sound in each word. Do not allow them to see the words or the book. This is an oral exercise.

- **Said**
- **Quilt**
- **List**
- **Squad**
- **Quail**
- **Quad**

Ask your student to isolate the **middle** sound in each word. Do not allow them to see the words or the book. This is an oral exercise.

- **Quite**
- **Dale**
- **Quack**
- **Queen**
- **Fate**
- **Seal**

Hear it

Isolating

Ask your student to isolate the **last** sound in each word. Do not allow them to see the words or the book. This is an oral exercise.

- **Quin**
- **Quod**
- **Quiz**
- **Quag**
- **Quiz**
- **Quip**

Hear it

Blending

Ask your student to blend the following sounds into words.

- **Qu-i-ll**
- **Qu-e-ll**
- **Qu-i-t**
- **Qu-i-n**
- **S-qu-a-d**
- **Qu-ai-l**

Segmenting

Ask your student to break apart the following words into sounds.

- **Aqua**
- **Squat**
- **Queen**
- **Squash**
- **Quack**
- **Quest**

189

Decode it

Word Reading

Ask your student to read the following words.

- Liquid
- Quick
- Quiz
- Squat
- Equip
- Quack

Sentence Reading

Ask your student to read the following sentences.

1. Jill will quilt a new quilt.
2. A quack was quick to quip.
3. The queen will quiz with us

Read it

Quin the queen had a big, soft quilt. One day, she sat on her quilt to do a quiz. A duck quack made the queen do a quick squat. The duck had lost its way. The queen led the duck back to the quiet pond. "Quack!" said the duck to quell the queen. The queen went back and sat on her quilt.

READ IT—THE 5 W'S (OPTIONAL)

Name: _____

Date: _____

Who?	
What?	
When?	
Where?	
Why?	

Read it

Silly Sentences

Ask your student to read the following nonsense words from the box below. Though these are not real words, the goal is to get students to read them fluently and quickly. To accomplish this, you student may try as many times as possible within 3-5 minutes.

1. **The quop quag on a quet.**
2. **Quib the quom with a quig.**
3. **A quag quit the quof quick.**
4. **Quibby quaps with a quog.**
5. **Quen quiz the quup for fun.**

Spell it

Ask your student to spell and write the following words:
Quin, Quiz, Quilt, Quell, Quack.

Spell it

Ask your student to write the word in the middle of the page on a white board. Then ask them to change the word into another word, making as few changes as possible. This will likely involve changing only one or two letters. Do not let them see this book while completing this exercise. Ex. Change "mat" into "cat". Change "cat" into "pat". Change "pat" into "pan". Change "pan" into "pad" Etc.

Squint

Squash

Squad

Squall

Squill

Digraph Qu

Set 3

Hear it

Isolating

Ask your student to isolate the **first** sound in each word. Do not allow them to see the words or the book. This is an oral exercise.

- **Squid**
- **Plum**
- **List**
- **Mint**
- **Squint**
- **Nine**

Ask your student to isolate the **middle** sound in each word. Do not allow them to see the words or the book. This is an oral exercise.

- **Nine**
- **Fame**
- **Quite**
- **Waste**
- **Ripe**
- **Gel**

Hear it

Isolating

Ask your student to isolate the **last** sound in each word. Do not allow them to see the words or the book. This is an oral exercise.

- **Squid**
- **Free**
- **Quirk**
- **Quiz**
- **Quail**
- **Squirm**

Hear it

Blending

Ask your student to blend the following sounds into words.

- **S-qu-all**
- **S-qu-i-n-t**
- **Qu-i-ck**
- **S-qu-i-d**
- **Qu-ir-k**
- **a-qu-a**

Segmenting

Ask your student to break apart the following words into sounds.

- **Squid**
- **Squall**
- **Aqua**
- **Quick**
- **Drill**
- **Flick**

Decode it

Word Reading

Ask your student to read the following words.

- **Squall**
- **Squint**
- **Quick**
- **Squid**
- **Quack**
- **aqua**

Sentence Reading

Ask your student to read the following sentences.

1. **The duck quacks by the squid.**
2. **A squid swims quick in the sea.**
3. **Quiz me on math and spelling.**

Read it

A squid lives in the quell aqua. It is quick and quiet. The squid swims fast to catch food. Fish swim in the liquid, and the squid gets one quick. A big fish swims by, and the squid quits. The squid rests in a quiet spot. The squid swims quick when the big fish swims away.

READ IT—THE 5 W'S (OPTIONAL)

Name: _____

Date: _____

Who?	
What?	
When?	
Where?	
Why?	

Read it

Silly Sentences

Ask your student to read the following nonsense words from the box below. Though these are not real words, the goal is to get students to read them fluently and quickly. To accomplish this, you student may try as many times as possible within 3-5 minutes.

1. **The quib quacks at the quop.**
2. **A quub quin the quex.**
3. **The quoz zips by the quid.**
4. **Quib and quok squill with quex.**
5. **Quid Quims a quub and a quox.**

Spell it

Ask your student to spell and write the following words: Squint, Squid, Liquid, Quick

--- --- --- --- --- ---

--- --- --- --- ---

--- --- --- --- --- ---

--- --- --- --- --- ---

Spell it

Ask your student to write the word in the middle of the page on a white board. Then ask them to change the word into another word, making as few changes as possible. This will likely involve changing only one or two letters. Do not let them see this book while completing this exercise. Ex. Change "mat" into "cat". Change "cat" into "pat". Change "pat" into "pan". Change "pan" into "pad" Etc.

Quick

Quip

Quiz

Quit

Quiet

Digraph Qu

Set 4

Hear it

Isolating

Ask your student to isolate the **first** sound in each word. Do not allow them to see the words or the book. This is an oral exercise.

- **Question**
- **Like**
- **Quill**
- **Girl**
- **Boy**
- **Quiz**

Ask your student to isolate the **middle** sound in each word. Do not allow them to see the words or the book. This is an oral exercise.

- **John**
- **Rile**
- **Quiz**
- **Aqua**
- **Quit**
- **Full**

Hear it

Isolating

Ask your student to isolate the **last** sound in each word. Do not allow them to see the words or the book. This is an oral exercise.

- **Quiz**
- **Question**
- **Quick**
- **Like**
- **Aqua**
- **Quid**

Hear it

Blending

Ask your student to blend the following sounds into words.

- **Qu-i-d**
- **Qu-i-z**
- **Qu-i-ll**
- **Quit**
- **Quip**
- **Quit**

Segmenting

Ask your student to break apart the following words into sounds.

- **Quill**
- **Quiz**
- **Quid**
- **Aqua**
- **Aqua**
- **Quick**

Decode it

Word Reading

Ask your student to read the following words.

- **Aqua**
- **Question**
- **Quiz**
- **Quit**
- **Quill**
- **Quid**

Sentence Reading

Ask your student to read the following sentences.

1. **Tom has a quiz.**
2. **Tom has a quill**
3. **He gets quid for the quiz.**

Read it

Tom has a quiz in class. He must quit talking and be quick. The quiz has math questions. He does the quiz with his quill for a quick quid from his mom. He sees a fun quiz question with a duck. The duck can quack and jump. Tom is glad to take the quiz. He works fast and is quiet. When he is done, he gets a quid from mom.

READ IT—THE 5 W'S (OPTIONAL)

Name: _____

Date: _____

Who?	
What?	
When?	
Where?	
Why?	

Read it
Silly Sentences

Ask your student to read the following nonsense words from the box below. Though these are not real words, the goal is to get students to read them fluently and quickly. To accomplish this, you student may try as many times as possible within 3-5 minutes.

1. **The quib jumps quiv the quax.**
2. **Quok and quip quan in the quib.**
3. **A quex runs past the quid.**
4. **The quop quet to the quix.**
5. **Quid and quab quad to the quix.**

Spell it
Ask your student to spell and write the following words:
Quiz, Quit, Quill, Quid, Quick

Spell it

Ask your student to write the word in the middle of the page on a white board. Then ask them to change the word into another word, making as few changes as possible. This will likely involve changing only one or two letters. Do not let them see this book while completing this exercise. Ex. Change "mat" into "cat". Change "cat" into "pat". Change "pat" into "pan". Change "pan" into "pad" Etc.

> ## Quit

Quiz

Quid

Quill

Quell

Digraph Qu
Set 5

Hear it

Isolating

Ask your student to isolate the **first** sound in each word. Do not allow them to see the words or the book. This is an oral exercise.

- Quest
- Quilt
- Quell
- liquid
- Quod

Ask your student to isolate the **middle** sound in each word. Do not allow them to see the words or the book. This is an oral exercise.

- Quod
- Hike
- Aqua
- Bat
- Cop
- Cope

Hear it

Isolating

Ask your student to isolate the **last** sound in each word. Do not allow them to see the words or the book. This is an oral **exercise**.

- **Quod**
- **Hike**
- **Aqua**
- **Bat**
- **Cop**
- **Cope**

Hear it

Blending

Ask your student to blend the following sounds into words.

- **Qu-o-d**
- **H-i-ke**
- **A-qu-a**
- **B-a-t**
- **C-o-p**
- **C-o-pe**

Segmenting

Ask your student to break apart the following words into sounds.

- **Quod**
- **Hike**
- **Aqua**
- **Bat**
- **Cop**
- **Cope**

Decode it
Word Reading

Ask your student to read the following words.

- **Liquid**
- **Aqua**
- **Quick**

- **Quest**
- **Quell**
- **Squad**

Sentence Reading

Ask your student to read the following sentences.

1. **An aqua fish swam in the pond.**
2. **The liquid squad is quell.**
3. **The aqua was tranquil.**

Read it

An aqua fish swam in the pond. It was quick and liked to play in the liquid. The fish met a duck and a frog. They all had fun in the aquatic. The fish would flip and flop. The water splashes. The liquid squad is quell in the quest for fun. The aqua was tranquil.

READ IT—THE 5 W'S (OPTIONAL)

Name: _____

Date: _____

Who?	
What?	
When?	
Where?	
Why?	

Read it
Silly Sentences

Ask your student to read the following nonsense words from the box below. Though these are not real words, the goal is to get students to read them fluently and quickly. To accomplish this, you student may try as many times as possible within 3-5 minutes.

1. **The quib quox quagged quick.**
2. **A quet quop met a quib.**
3. **Quen quit the quif with quaf.**
4. **The quim quiz the quup.**
5. **Quop and quet went to the quib.**

Spell it

Ask your student to spell and
write the following words:
Aqua, Aquatic, Liquid,

- - - - -

- - - - - - - -

- - - - - - -

Spell it

Ask your student to write the word in the middle of the page on a white board. Then ask them to change the word into another word, making as few changes as possible. This will likely involve changing only one or two letters. Do not let them see this book while completing this exercise. Ex. Change "mat" into "cat". Change "cat" into "pat". Change "pat" into "pan". Change "pan" into "pad" Etc.

Quid

Quiz

Quick

Quill

Quilt

Digraph Wh
Set 1

Hear it

Isolating

Ask your student to isolate the **first** sound in each word. Do not allow them to see the words or the book. This is an oral exercise.

- **What**
- **Late**
- **Whip**
- **Right**
- **Wham**
- **Whiz**

Ask your student to isolate the **middle** sound in each word. Do not allow them to see the words or the book. This is an oral exercise.

- **Whap**
- **Whit**
- **Whup**
- **When**
- **Whig**
- **Whid**

Hear it

Isolating

Ask your student to isolate the **last** sound in each word. Do not allow them to see the words or the book. This is an oral exercise.

- **Whip**
- **Will**
- **Why**
- **Wait**
- **Whoa**
- **Whew**

Hear it

Blending

Ask your student to blend the following sounds into words.

- **Wh-a-t**
- **Wh-e-n**
- **Wh-i-p**
- **Wh-i-m**
- **Wh-a-m**
- **Wh-i-z**

Segmenting

Ask your student to break apart the following words into sounds.

- **Whap**
- **Whit**
- **Whup**
- **Whee**
- **Whim**
- **Who**

Decode it

Word Reading

Ask your student to read the following words.

- **Whip**
- **When**
- **Why**
- **Who**
- **Whew**
- **Whiz**

Sentence Reading

Ask your student to read the following sentences.

1. **What can we whip up?**
2. **When will she whiz by?**
3. **Whip the top, then spin.**

Read it

Whip the top with a thin, long whip. When you whip, the top will spin fast. What fun to watch it whiz! Whit had a whip and liked to play. He whipped the top in the yard. Wham! The top hit a wall and fell. Whit picked it up and tried again. Whip the top when you can!

READ IT—THE 5 W'S (OPTIONAL)

Name: _____

Date: _____

Who?	
What?	
When?	
Where?	
Why?	

Read it

Silly Sentences

Ask your student to read the following nonsense words from the box below. Though these are not real words, the goal is to get students to read them fluently and quickly. To accomplish this, you student may try as many times as possible within 3-5 minutes.

1. **Whop the wib, and whud the fop!**
2. **Whim the zix, then whot the plo.**
3. **Whug the dox, but whin the jup.**
4. **Whap the gev, whill whut the mib.**
5. **Whab the zon, then whid the wax.**

Spell it

Ask your student to spell and write the following words: What, When, Whip, Whiz, Which.

Spell it

Ask your student to write the word in the middle of the page on a white board. Then ask them to change the word into another word, making as few changes as possible. This will likely involve changing only one or two letters. Do not let them see this book while completing this exercise. Ex. Change "mat" into "cat". Change "cat" into "pat". Change "pat" into "pan". Change "pan" into "pad" Etc.

Why

What

Whip

Whit

Wham

Digraph Wh
Set 2

Hear it

Isolating

Ask your student to isolate the **first** sound in each word. Do not allow them to see the words or the book. This is an oral exercise.

- **Slip**
- **Which**
- **Wham**
- **Zoo**
- **Take**
- **Whiz**

Ask your student to isolate the **middle** sound in each word. Do not allow them to see the words or the book. This is an oral exercise.

- **Whim**
- **What**
- **Wheat**
- **Bill**
- **Whig**
- **When**

Hear it

Isolating

Ask your student to isolate the **last** sound in each word. Do not allow them to **see the** words or the **book**. This is an oral **exercise**.

- **Whom**
- **Why**
- **Whoa**
- **Whiff**
- **Whisk**
- **When**

Hear it

Blending

Ask your student to blend the following sounds into words.

- **Wh-i-ch**
- **Wh-i-s-k**
- **Wh-a-t**
- **Wh-y**
- **Wh-i-ff**
- **Wh-i-p**

Segmenting

Ask your student to break apart the following words into sounds.

- **Whim**
- **Whit**
- **Whig**
- **Whip**
- **White**
- **When**

Decode it

Word Reading

Ask your student to read the following words.

- **Whup**
- **Whit**
- **Whom**
- **Whig**
- **Why**
- **Whip**

Sentence Reading

Ask your student to read the following sentences.

1. **The dog whips the toy.**
2. **She will wham the bug.**
3. **I can whiz fast.**

Read it

Whale was in the whimsy sea. It whisks and whips. When Whale swam, fish hid. Whale went to a ship. The ship was white. Whale saw a man on the ship. Whale whips and whams. The man got wet. Whale liked to swim and play. Which the man did not like. What a fun day for Whale! The man whiff's the whale and goes home.

READ IT—THE 5 W'S (OPTIONAL)

Name: _____

Date: _____

Who?	
What?	
When?	
Where?	
Why?	

Read it
Silly Sentences

Ask your student to read the following nonsense words from the box below. Though these are not real words, the goal is to get students to read them fluently and quickly. To accomplish this, you student may try as many times as possible within 3-5 minutes.

1. **Whox whed and wham fled.**
2. **whiff ziff and whoff rol.**
3. **whem whet and whec whad.**
4. **Whas whep and whum whim.**
5. **Whud whax and whusk fom**

Spell it

Ask your student to spell and write the following words: Whip, Whim, Whiz, Whit, Wham.

Spell it

Ask your student to write the word in the middle of the page on a white board. Then ask them to change the word into another word, making as few changes as possible. This will likely involve changing only one or two letters. Do not let them see this book while completing this exercise. Ex. Change "mat" into "cat". Change "cat" into "pat". Change "pat" into "pan". Change "pan" into "pad" Etc.

> **Whiz**

Wham

Whim

When

What

Digraph Wh

Set 3

Hear it

Isolating

Ask your student to isolate the **first** sound in each word. Do not allow them to see the words or the book. This is an oral exercise.

- **Whiff**
- **While**
- **Right**
- **Each**
- **At**
- **Whip**

Ask your student to isolate the **middle** sound in each word. Do not allow them to see the words or the book. This is an oral exercise.

- **Whig**
- **Whup**
- **Fill**
- **Veal**
- **Leap**
- **Cube**

Hear it

Isolating

Ask your student to isolate the **last** sound in each word. Do not allow them to see the words or the book. This is an oral exercise.

- **Who**
- **Why**
- **Will**

- **Whos**
- **Whale**
- **White**

Hear it

Blending

Ask your student to blend the following sounds into words.

- **Wh-o**
- **Wh-y**
- **Wh-a-m**
- **Wh-a-t**
- **Wh-e-n**
- **Wh-i-t-e**

Segmenting

Ask your student to break apart the following words into sounds.

- **White**
- **Whale**
- **Whee**
- **Whip**
- **Will**
- **Whom**

Decode it

Word Reading

Ask your student to read the following words.

- **Whop**
- **Whit**
- **Whom**
- **Whif**
- **Whir**
- **Wham**

Sentence Reading

Ask your student to read the following sentences.

1. **What did she whip?**
2. **When will he whiz by?**
3. **Wham! The whip hit.**

Read it

Whiz is a kid who loves to play. He can whip by fast on his white bike. One day, Whiz went to the park. When he got there, he saw a big hill. "What a whim!" Whiz said. He rode up the hill and went left with a whiz. "Who is that? Why is does he whip on a whim?", Whitman said. But Whiz just had fun.

READ IT—THE 5 W'S (OPTIONAL)

Name: _____

Date: _____

Who?	
What?	
When?	
Where?	
Why?	

Read it
Silly Sentences

Ask your student to read the following nonsense words from the box below. Though these are not real words, the goal is to get students to read them fluently and quickly. To accomplish this, you student may try as many times as possible within 3-5 minutes.

1. **Whil whon whith whed.**
2. **Whov whec whon whod.**
3. **Whag whod whon whim.**
4. **Whill wheff whos and whed.**
5. **Whis Whuff whip whun.**

Spell it

Ask your student to spell and write the following words: Whim, whip, what, whiz, Whitman.

_____ _____ _____ _____

_____ _____ _____ _____

_____ _____ _____ _____

_____ _____ _____ _____

____ ____ ____ ____ ____

Spell it

Ask your student to write the word in the middle of the page on a white board. Then ask them to change the word into another word, making as few changes as possible. This will likely involve changing only one or two letters. Do not let them see this book while completing this exercise. Ex. Change "mat" into "cat". Change "cat" into "pat". Change "pat" into "pan". Change "pan" into "pad" Etc.

Why

Who

When

Whip

What

Digraph Wh
Set 4

Hear it

Isolating

Ask your student to isolate the **first** sound in each word. Do not allow them to see the words or the book. This is an oral exercise.

- **Gill**
- **Why**
- **Yes**
- **No**
- **Whip**
- **Vail**

Ask your student to isolate the **middle** sound in each word. Do not allow them to see the words or the book. This is an oral exercise.

- **Whom**
- **Whit**
- **Wham**
- **Whop**
- **Will**
- **Yes**

Hear it

Isolating

Ask your student to isolate the **last** sound in each word. Do not allow them to see the words or the book. This is an oral exercise.

- **Why**
- **Who**
- **What**
- **Whiz**
- **Which**
- **Whack**

Hear it

Blending

Ask your student to blend the following sounds into words.

- **Who**
- **why**
- **when**
- **what**
- **whip**
- **whiz**

Segmenting

Ask your student to break apart the following words into sounds.

- **whom**
- **whet**
- **wham**
- **whop**
- **whee**
- **whig**

Decode it

Word Reading

Ask your student to read the following words.

- **whom**
- **whet**
- **wham**
- **whin**
- **whap**
- **whiz**

Sentence Reading

Ask your student to read the following sentences.

1. **Why did she go on a whim?**
2. **What a whip!**
3. **When will the whale go by?**

Read it

"Who is that?" Whip said when he saw the whiz kid. "What can you do?" he asked. The whiz kid had a big box. He said, "Which whimsy do you want? The box or the whip?" He took out a whip and had it whiz. Whip said, "Wow! what was that?" The whiz kid said, "Thanks! You can try it too."

READ IT-THE 5 W'S (OPTIONAL)

Name: _____

Date: _____

Who?	
What?	
When?	
Where?	
Why?	

Read it
Silly Sentences

Ask your student to read the following nonsense words from the box below. Though these are not real words, the goal is to get students to read them fluently and quickly. To accomplish this, you student may try as many times as possible within 3-5 minutes.

1. **Whap the whel and it wizz.**
2. **Whit the wock and whum it.**
3. **Whiz whad the whut?**
4. **Whig the whup on the wex.**
5. **Wham whod the whip Whut?**

Spell it

Ask your student to spell and write the following words:
Who, Why, What, When, Whiz

Spell it

Ask your student to write the word in the middle of the page on a white board. Then ask them to change the word into another word, making as few changes as possible. This will likely involve changing only one or two letters. Do not let them see this book while completing this exercise. Ex. Change "mat" into "cat". Change "cat" into "pat". Change "pat" into "pan". Change "pan" into "pad" Etc.

When

What

Wham

Whiz

Whip

Digraph Wh

Set 5

Hear it

Isolating

Ask your student to isolate the **first** sound in each word. Do not allow them to see the words or the book. This is an oral exercise.

- **Whiz**
- **Beam**
- **Riff**
- **Page**
- **Jake**
- **Wax**

Ask your student to isolate the **middle** sound in each word. Do not allow them to see the words or the book. This is an oral exercise.

- **Wipe**
- **Juice**
- **Will**
- **Zoo**
- **Farm**
- **Wet**

Hear it

Isolating

Ask your student to isolate the **last** sound in each word. Do not allow them to see the words or the book. This is an oral exercise.

- **While**
- **Whiff**
- **Win**
- **Dill**
- **Sail**
- **Won**

Hear it

Blending

Ask your student to blend the following sounds into words.

- **Wh-ee-l**
- **Wh-a-m**
- **Wh-a-ck**

- **Wh-i-p**
- **Wh-o-p**
- **Wh-e-n**

Segmenting

Ask your student to break apart the following words into sounds.

- **Wheel**
- **Wham**
- **Whack**

- **Whip**
- **Whop**
- **When**

Decode it
Word Reading

Ask your student to read the following words.

- **Wh-ee-l**
- **Wh-a-m**
- **Wh-a-ck**
- **Wh-i-p**
- **Wh-o-p**
- **Wh-e-n**

Sentence Reading

Ask your student to read the following sentences.

1. **Who has the whip?**
2. **When did Whit get the wheel?**
3. **What is that with Zack?**

Read it

Whit had a big wheel. The wheel had a whiz sound. Whit went up the hill with the wheel. The wheel hit a rock and went "Wham! Whack!" Whit was sad. Then, Whit's pal, Jan, went to help. They got the wheel and went up the hill when they could.

READ IT—THE 5 W'S (OPTIONAL)

Name: _____

Date: _____

Who?	
What?	
When?	
Where?	
Why?	

Read it
Silly Sentences

Ask your student to read the following nonsense words from the box below. Though these are not real words, the goal is to get students to read them fluently and quickly. To accomplish this, you student may try as many times as possible within 3-5 minutes.

1. **Whib whum a whod.**
2. **Whal whup in the wham.**
3. **Whop whig on a whax.**
4. **Whut whes by the whag.**
5. **Whid whol with a whig.**

Spell it

Ask your student to spell and write the following words: Wheel, Whitman, Whiz, Wham.

Spell it

Ask your student to write the word in the middle of the page on a white board. Then ask them to change the word into another word, making as few changes as possible. This will likely involve changing only one or two letters. Do not let them see this book while completing this exercise. Ex. Change "mat" into "cat". Change "cat" into "pat". Change "pat" into "pan". Change "pan" into "pad" Etc.

Whup

What

When

Whin

Whet

Made in the USA
Las Vegas, NV
28 August 2024